Short and Long Vowels

W9-BBY-102

Written by

Kim Cernek and Vicky Shiotsu

Editor: Stacey Faulkner
Illustrators: Jenny Campbell and Darcy Tom
Cover Illustrator: Rick Grayson
Designer: The Development Source
Art Director: Moonhee Pak
Project Director: Betsy Morris

Table of Contents

Introduction

About the Build-a-Skill Instant Books Series

The *Build-a-Skill Instant Books* series features a variety of reproducible instant books that focus on important reading and math skills covered in the primary classroom. Each instant book is easy to make, and once children become familiar with the basic formats that appear throughout the series, they will be able to make new books with little help. Children will love the unique, manipulative quality of the books and will want to read them over and over again as they gain mastery of basic learning skills!

About the Build-a-Skill Instant Books: Short and Long Vowels

This book helps children identify short and long vowel sounds through fun and easy-to-make instant books. Children will develop fine motor skills and practice following directions as they cut, fold, and staple the reproducible pages together to make flip books, step books, and word wallets. As children read and reread their instant books, they will strengthen their decoding skills and increase their sight word vocabulary.

Refer to the Table of Contents to help with lesson planning. Choose instant book activities that fit with current curriculum goals in your regular or ELL classroom. Use the instant books to practice skills or introduce new ones. Directions for making the instant books appear on pages 3 and 4. These should be copied and sent along with the book patterns when assigning a bookmaking activity as homework.

Making and Using the Instant Books

All of the instant books in this resource require only one or two pieces of paper. Copy the pages on white copy paper or card stock, or use colored paper to jazz up and vary the formats. Children will love personalizing their instant books by coloring them, adding construction paper covers, or decorating them with collage materials such as wiggly eyes, ribbon, and stickers. Customize the instant books by adding extra pages, or by creating your own word cards.

Children can make instant books as an enrichment activity when their regular classwork is done, as a learning center activity during guided reading time, or as a homework assignment. They can place completed instant books in their classroom book boxes and then read and reread the books independently or with a reading buddy. After children have had many opportunities to read their books in school, send the books home for extra skill-building practice. Encourage children to store the books in a special box that they have labeled "I Can Read Box."

Directions for Making the Instant Books

There are three basic formats for the instant books in this guide. The directions appear below for quick and easy reference. The directions are written *to* the child, in case you would like to send the bookmaking activities home as homework. Just copy the directions and attach them to the instant book pages.

Flip Book (set 1), pages 5, 6, 7, 8, 9, 10, 11, 12, 13, 14

1. Finish the book by tracing the letters.
2. Cut out the flip book and word cards.
3. Staple the word cards to the flip book.
4. "Flip up" each card to practice reading your words.

Step Book, pages 15–16 and 17–18

1. Cut out the five boxes.
2. Put the pages in order with the smallest square on top.
3. Staple the pages at the top to make a book.
4. Say the names of the vowels and pictures.

Optional: Color the pictures.

Word Wallet, pages 19–20, 21–22, 23–24, 25–26

1. Trace the dotted letters on the wallet.
2. Cut out the wallet.
3. Fold it in half along the solid middle line.
4. Staple where shown. Tape the outer edges. Fold the wallet closed.
5. Cut out the word cards. Sort them into the correct pockets.

Flip Book (set 2), pages 27, 28, 29, 30, 31, 32

1. Cut out the flip book and word cards.
2. Staple the word cards to the flip book.
3. Read each word. Say if the **vowel sound** is short or long.

Build-a-Skill Instant Books • Short and Long Vowels © 2015 Creative Teaching Press

Short a Flip Book

I can read

Staple word cards here.

I can read | short **a**

can

rat

map

ham

bag

sad

Short e Flip Book

Staple word cards here.

I can read | short **e**

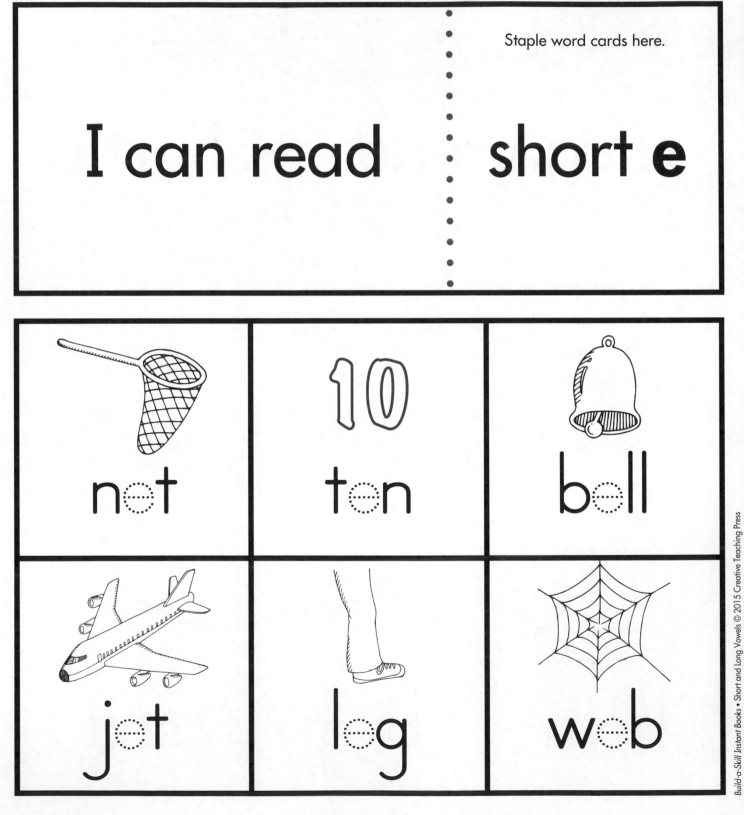

net

ten

bell

jet

leg

web

Build-a-Skill Instant Books • Short and Long Vowels © 2015 Creative Teaching Press

I can read

I can read : short i

Staple word cards here.

ship

dish

bib

hill

chick

lid

Short o Flip Book

I can read
Pot

Staple word cards here.

I can read | short **o**

pot

clock

hop

doll

box

stop

Build-a-Skill Instant Books • Short and Long Vowels • © 2015 Creative Teaching Press

Short u Flip Book

I can read duck

Staple word cards here.

I can read   short **u**

bus

run

gum

cut

rug

duck

Long a Flip Book

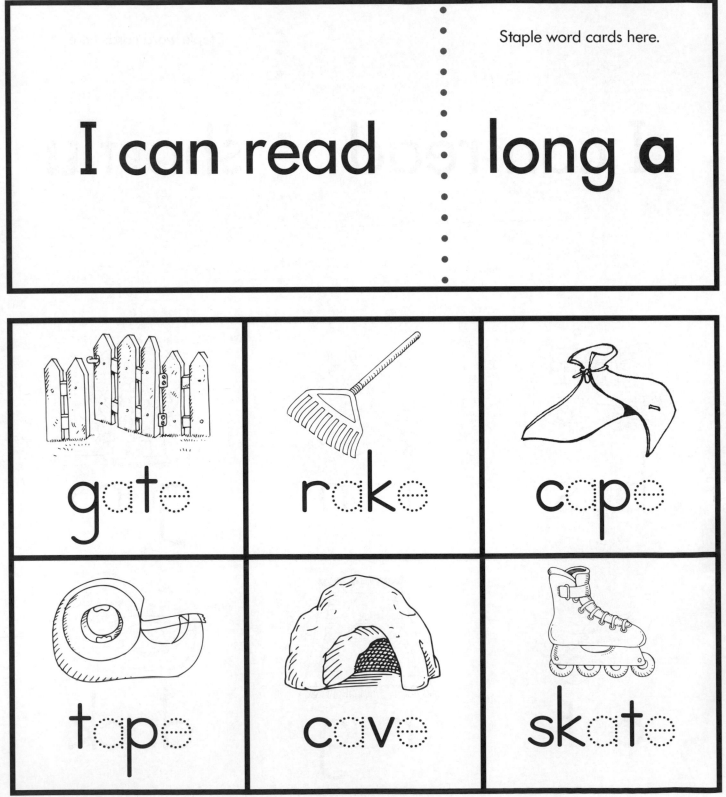

I can read long **a**

Staple word cards here.

gate

rake

cape

tape

cave

skate

Build-a-Skill Instant Books • Short and Long Vowels © 2015 Creative Teaching Press

Long e Flip Book

Staple word cards here.

I can read · long **e**

sheep

bean

seal

meat

read

seed

Build-a-Skill Instant Books • Short and Long Vowels © 2015 Creative Teaching Press

Long i Flip Book

I can read

Staple word cards here.

I can read | long **i**

pile

dime

dice

vine

slide

prize

Build-a-Skill Instant Books • Short and Long Vowels © 2015 Creative Teaching Press

Long o Flip Book

I can read bone

I can read | long o

Staple word cards here.

rose

hose

note

robe

bone

nose

Long u Flip Book

I can read

Staple word cards here.

I can read | long **u**

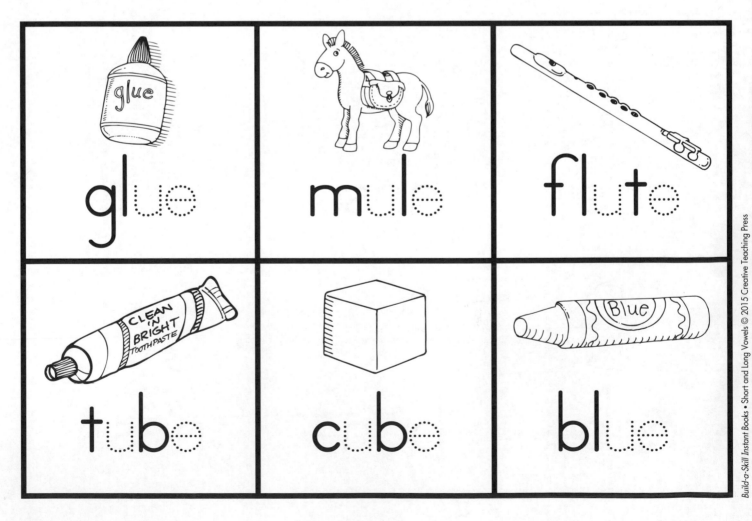

glue

mule

flute

tube

cube

blue

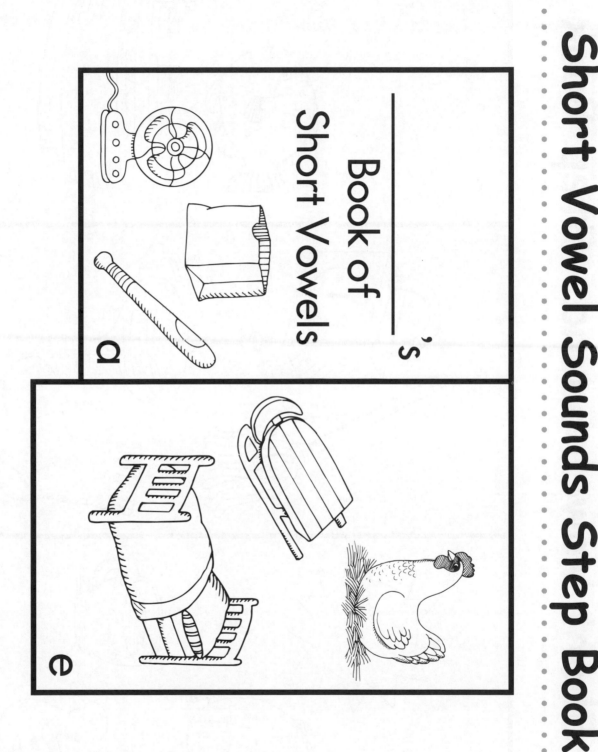

Book of
_____'s
Short Vowels

a

e

Short Vowel Sounds Step Book

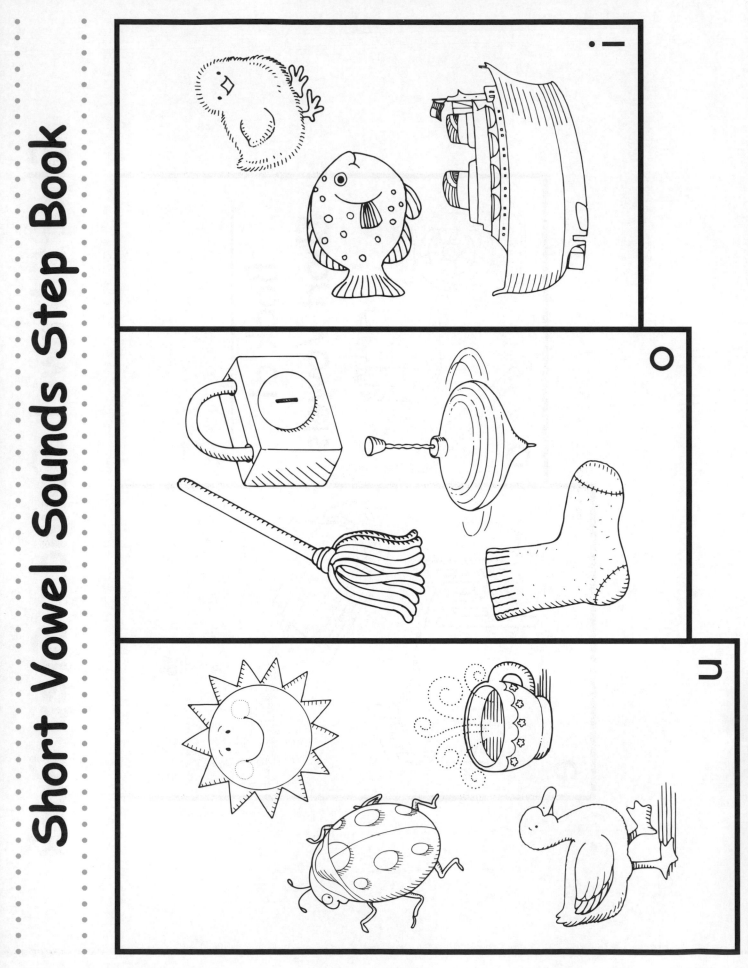

Build-a-Skill Instant Books • Short and Long Vowels © 2015 Creative Teaching Press

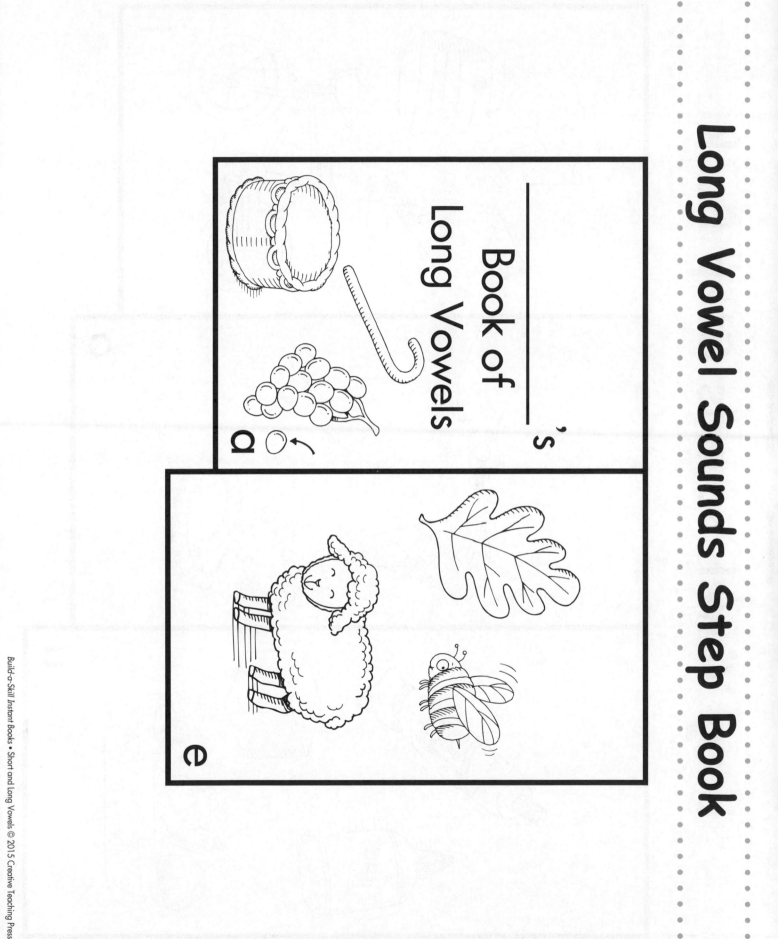

Book of _____'s
Long Vowels

a

e

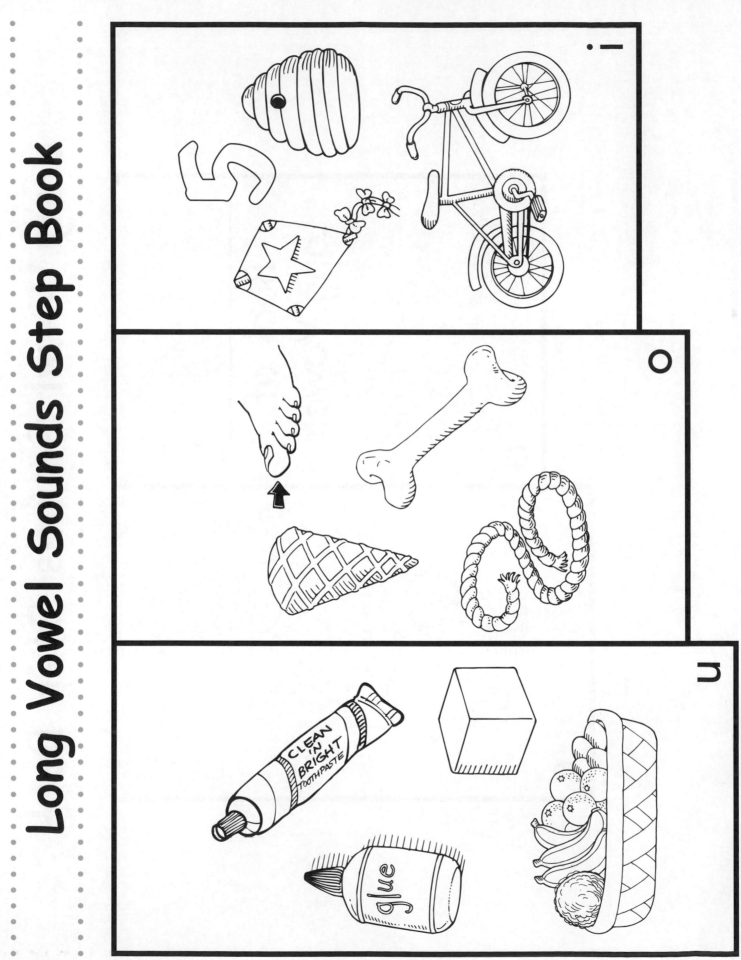

Build-a-Skill Instant Books • Short and Long Vowels © 2015 Creative Teaching Press

a, e, i

Short __a__ Words

Short __e__ Words

Short __i__ Words

Word Wallet

's

Tape here.

Staple here.

Staple here.

Tape here.

Fold here.

Tape here.

Wallet Words: Short a, e, i

Build-a-Skill Instant Books • Short and Long Vowels © 2015 Creative Teaching Press

i, o, u

Short _i_ Words

Short _o_ Words

Short _u_ Words

Word Wallet

_____'s

Tape here.

Tape here.

Tape here.

Tape here.

Staple here.

Staple here.

Fold here.

Wallet Words: Short i, o, u

Build-a-Skill Instant Books • Short and Long Vowels © 2015 Creative Teaching Press

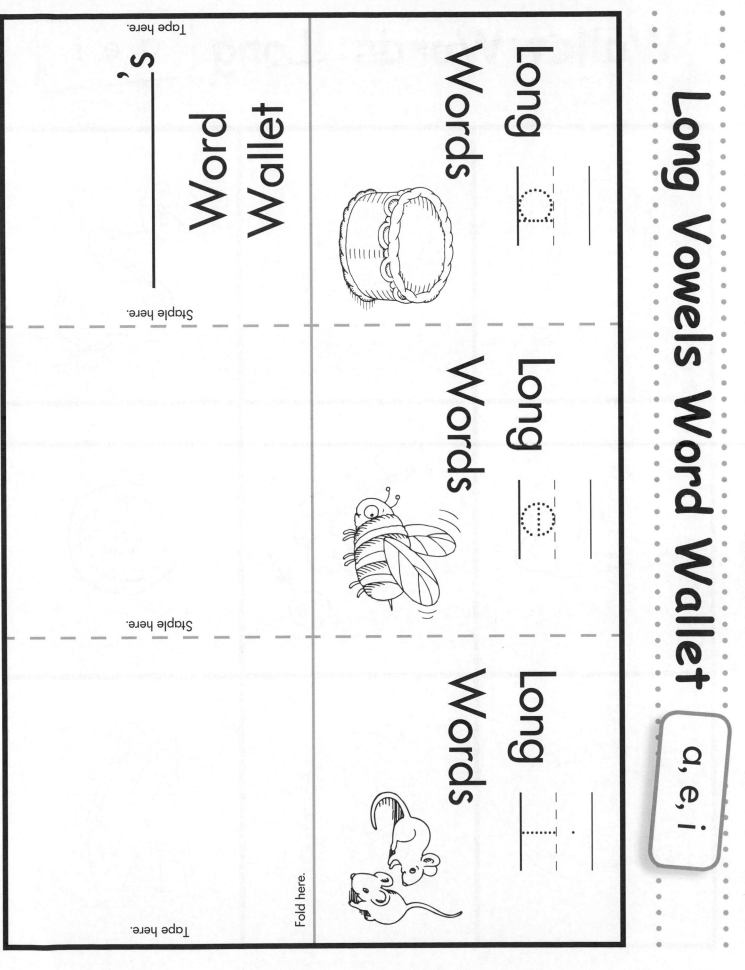

Long Vowels Word Wallet

a, e, i

Long __o__ Words

Long __e__ Words

Long __i__ Words

Word Wallet

's

Tape here.

Staple here.

Staple here.

Tape here.

Fold here.

Tape here.

Build-a-Skill Instant Books • Short and Long Vowels © 2015 Creative Teaching Press

Wallet Words: Long a, e, i

Build-a-Skill Instant Books • Short and Long Vowels © 2015 Creative Teaching Press

i, o, u

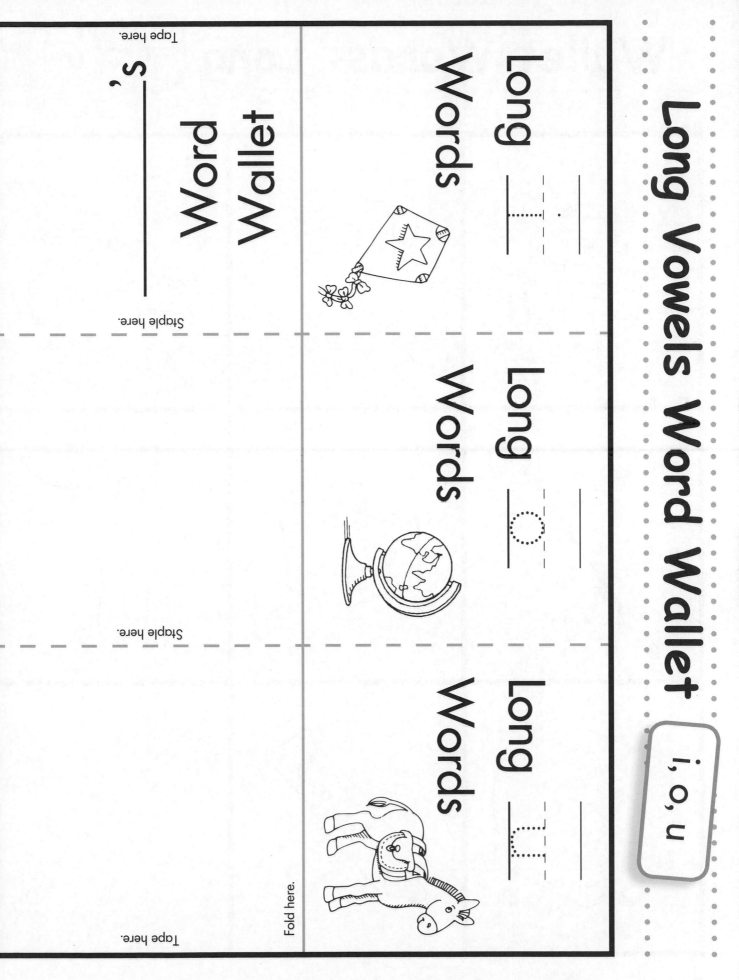

Long
Words

Word
Wallet

Long
Words

's

Tape here.

Staple here.

Staple here.

Tape here.

Long
Words

Long
Words

Fold here.

Tape here.

Wallet Words: Long i, o, u

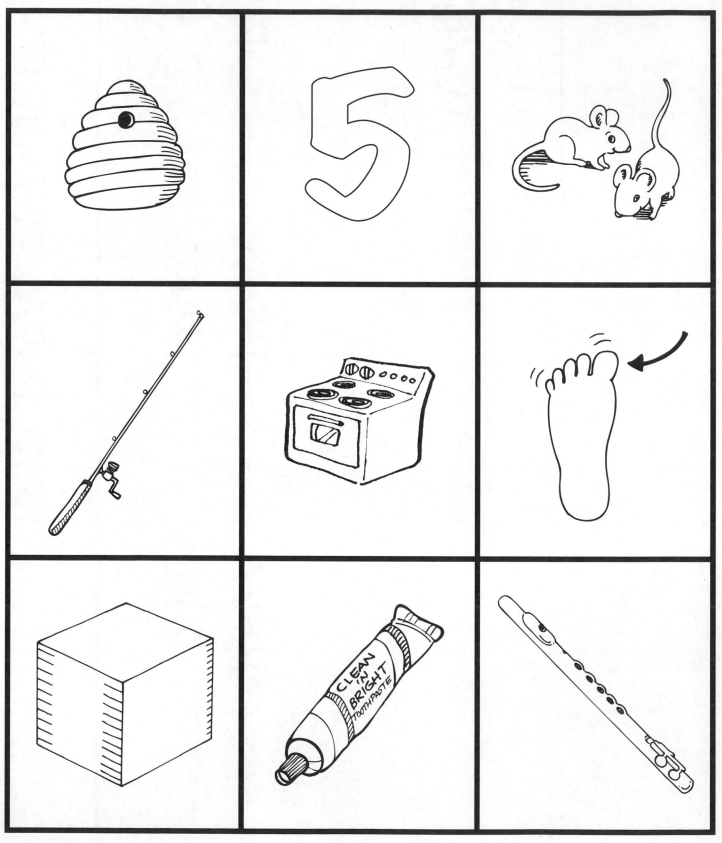

Build-a-Skill Instant Books • Short and Long Vowels © 2015 Creative Teaching Press

Watch Me Read! Flip Book

Staple cards here.

Watch Me Read!

can	tap	mat
cane	tape	mate
bit	fin	rob
bite	fine	robe
hop	cut	cub
hope	cute	cube

Build-a-Skill Instant Books • Short and Long Vowels © 2015 Creative Teaching Press

Two Sounds of a Flip Book

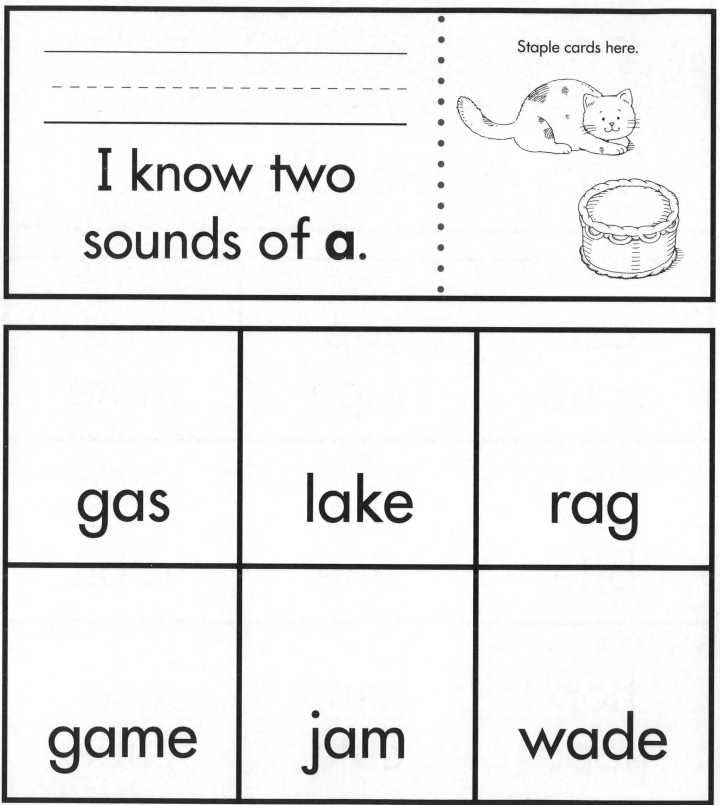

I know two sounds of **a**.

Staple cards here.

gas	lake	rag
game	jam	wade

Build-a-Skill Instant Books • Short and Long Vowels © 2015 Creative Teaching Press

Two Sounds of e Flip Book

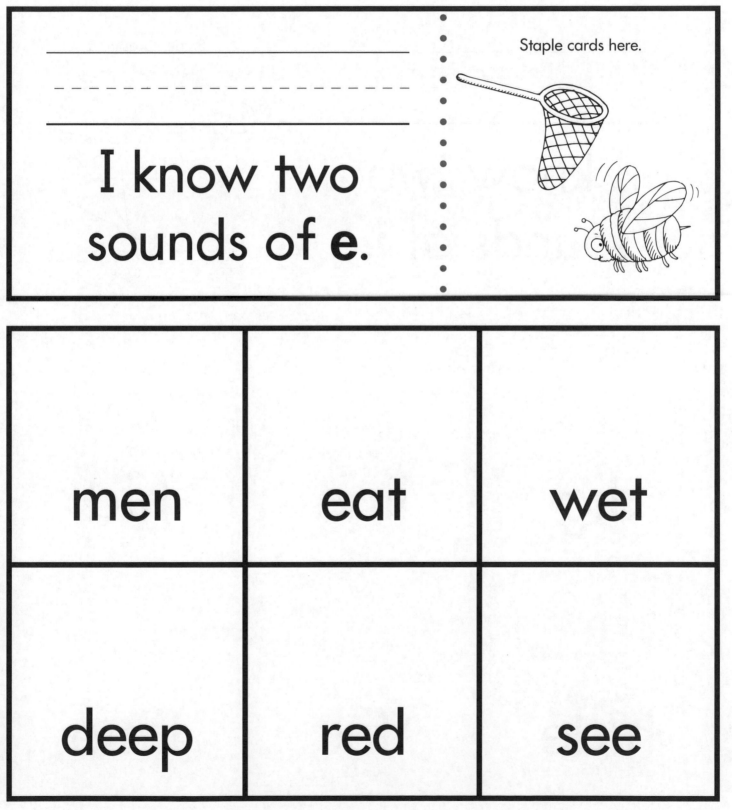

Staple cards here.

I know two
sounds of **e**.

men	eat	wet
deep	red	see

Build-a-Skill Instant Books • Short and Long Vowels © 2015 Creative Teaching Press

Two Sounds of i Flip Book

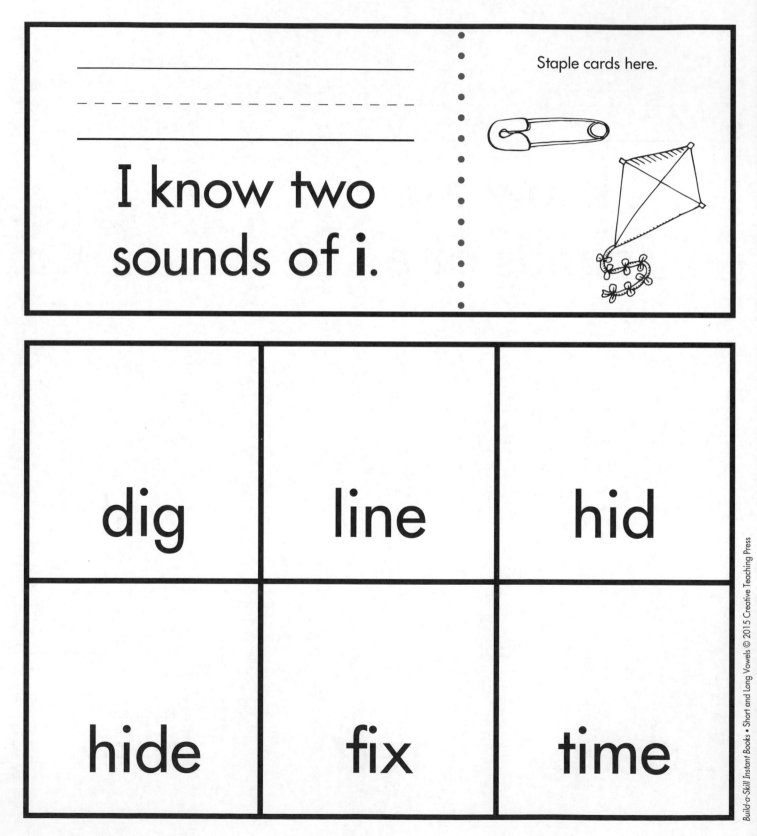

_____
- - - - - - - - - - - - - - - -
_____

I know two sounds of **i**.

Staple cards here.

dig	line	hid
hide	fix	time

Build-a-Skill Instant Books • Short and Long Vowels © 2015 Creative Teaching Press

Two Sounds of o Flip Book

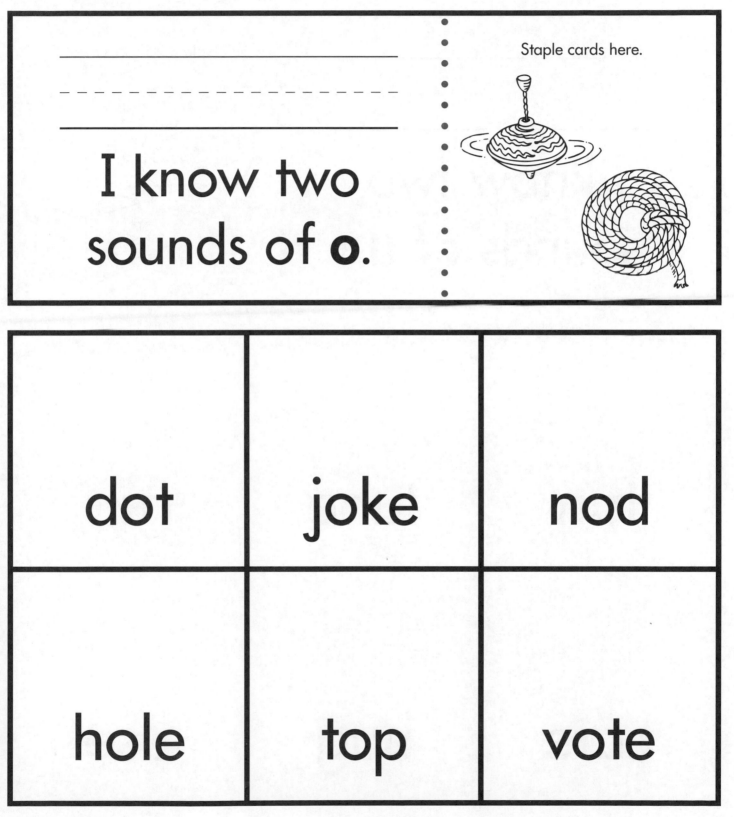

Staple cards here.

I know two sounds of **o**.

dot	joke	nod
hole	top	vote

Two Sounds of u Flip Book

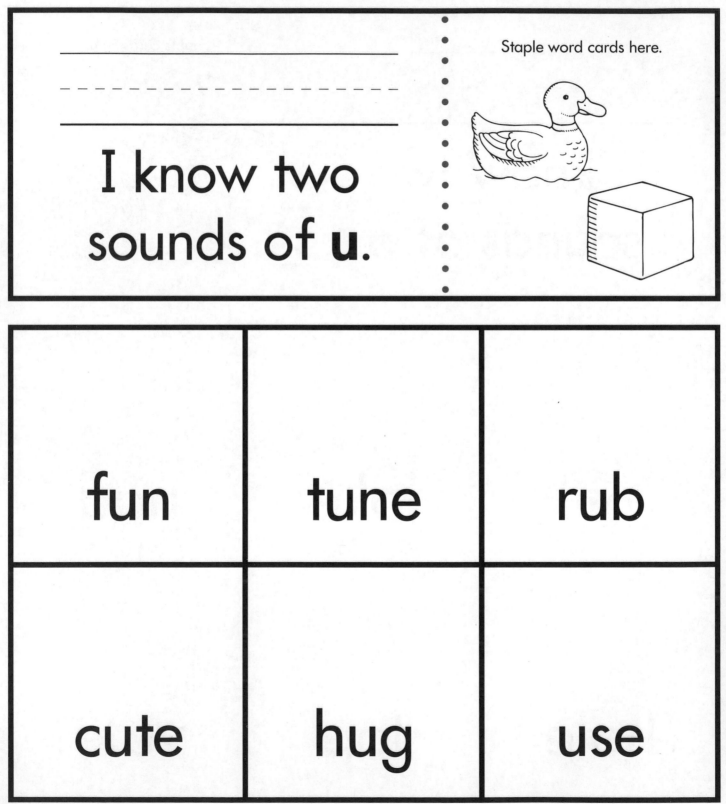

_____

- - - - - - - - - -

_____

I know two sounds of **u**.

Staple word cards here.

fun	tune	rub
cute	hug	use

Build-a-Skill Instant Books • Short and Long Vowels © 2015 Creative Teaching Press